The

Computer Athlete's

Handbook

Your Guide to a Healthier,
Happier Techy Lifestyle

Brian Bentow

The Computer Athlete's Handbook:
Your Guide to a Happier, Healthier Techy Lifestyle

Computer Athlete Media
Post Office Box 687
Princeton Junction, NJ 08550

www.computerathlete.net

ISBN: 978-0-9820447-0-4

2008907570

To everyone and anyone

who will ever use a computer

Brian Bentow

Table of Contents

Introduction

Do you currently have a less-than-comfortable computer setup, back or hand pain, poor habits, or a stressful work environment? If so, unless you make some changes to your habits or work environment, you are destined for repetitive stress injuries.

Unfortunately, most people are either not aware of, or simply take no steps to avoid, the painful problems that await them. It is akin to a man who jumps off a 40-story building and, as he passes the 10th floor, says, "I'm doing fine. I haven't hit the ground yet!"

The good news is that this book can help you remove the pain from your computer usage by showing you how to take on the techniques and perspective of what I call a "computer athlete." In this book, you will find cost-effective ways to gradually improve your computing habits and environment, eventually achieving a pain-free computing experience.

The computer athlete's perspective can guide your everyday decisions. For example, when deciding whether to eat a donut for breakfast, you can ask yourself, "Would a computer athlete eat this for breakfast?" Your answer will be clear: "I don't think so." As a computer athlete, you can become a happy, healthy computer user who focuses on and accomplishes goals in a manner that is sustainable throughout your life.

If by reading this book you can avoid even a single pointless doctor's visit, the investment of time and money will have more than paid for itself. The cost of this book will pay for itself many times over by enabling you to work longer hours without pain and become more productive, helping you purchase the right equipment for your needs, and in many cases providing you with the incalculable benefit of saving you from a debilitating injury that could force you to change careers.

The computer athlete model has enabled me to work 12 to 15 hours a day, six to seven days a week, for several years, in such settings as my computer-intensive undergraduate career at Harvey Mudd College, internships at Microsoft, side jobs and side projects, and most recently working at a software startup company as the Lead Software Developer/Manager of Product Development/Software Architect/Technical Specialist. The techniques that I have developed have served me well even under incredibly intense, sink-or-swim work conditions.

The way the tips and techniques described in this book will apply to you will vary with your situation: usage patterns, work obligations, work environment, aspirations, needs, work schedules, and so on. For example, many junior analyst investment bankers use Microsoft Excel heavily. They work long hours and need to press the Control, Shift, and Function keys frequently. These repetitive keystrokes and the awkward hand positions they require cause repetitive stress injuries. On the other hand, many of the principles and techniques that a junior analyst would use will also be relevant to other types of computer users.

I have helped people in many different lines of work with their computer pain through the computer athlete model.

I chose to share my idea of the computer athlete after reading Jim and Michele McCarthy's slogan, "All live in greatness," and doing some reflection. I very much believe in promoting that idea. I believe that in order to live in greatness, I need to help others live in greatness. For example, if a large number of people are unable to work due to computer-related injuries, fewer problems will be solved, and we will all be worse off. I have been able to accomplish a considerable amount in a short period of time through hard work and motivation, as well as by developing the idea of and striving to become a computer athlete. I believe that there are many other individuals who will be able to do likewise. Even if you only want to use the computer without pain for a few hours a day, this book can help you get there.

I have boiled the model for becoming a computer athlete down to the mastering of five key disciplinary areas: **Equipment and Usage, Nutrition, Self-Awareness and**

Self-Care, Strength and Conditioning, and Stress Management. This book discusses each of these areas in depth and explains why mastering each one is critical for reaching a state of pain-free computing.

1. My Story

I started using a computer regularly at the age of ten. Throughout middle school and high school, I used a computer to play computer games, instant message my friends, and complete homework assignments. I now know that I had poor posture, poor equipment, and poor habits. At that time, I had little knowledge of ergonomics and had had no formal training in computer use. My setup was pretty typical; it was nothing special. I had a standard mouse; a standard keyboard (I didn't even have a natural keyboard); an uncomfortable, inexpensive task chair; and a 17" CRT monitor. Although I did not experience any memorable pain during that time, that was about to change.

During my first Computer Science course at Harvey Mudd College, I developed the beginnings of carpal tunnel syndrome. Because assistance was more accessible in the computer lab in the computer science department, I would do most of my programming work there. Unfortunately, the computer lab had an awful computing environment: it had terrible, unsteady chairs; table tops set at a poor height; antiquated mouses and keyboards; and did not allow food or drinks. I was also using Emacs as my text editor, which required quite a bit of Shift-Control key commands. Over the course of the semester, I found myself beset by wrist pain, numbness, cold fingers, and other symptoms of carpal tunnel. I became very concerned.

At that point, I sought the advice of some of the physical trainers at the college gym. One of the trainers told me to take breaks, ice my wrists, and wear wrist braces at night. Looking back, that advice was not terrible, but it was just the tip of the iceberg compared to the adjustments that I would eventually need to make. Fortunately, I decided to ask for help and spoke to some of my professors in the Computer Science Department. I found out that one professor had worked in the private sector for many years and had been dealing with computer-related injuries for ten years. His advice was to use wrist braces only at night if at all, because over the long term they would lead to the weakening of stabilizer muscles in your arm. He also recommended using a foot pedal, which is a device that can be configured to press any keys you want and/or to change text editors. The idea of using a foot pedal interested me, but it seemed a bit extreme at the time. Until the end of the semester, I minimized the amount of time that I spent on the computer; worked mostly from my dorm room, which had a better setup; and iced my wrists. The semester ended and the pain gradually went away, so I ignored the problem for the time being.

Roughly one year later, during my sophomore year, things took a big turn for the worse. My financial aid dried up because my sister had graduated from college and my expected family contribution doubled, a situation which I did not have the foresight to anticipate. My parents and I had arranged that they would pay no more than $20,000 per year for four years toward my college education. During my college years, the annual cost of attending college went from around $34,000 to $40,000 per year. While my tuition increased by 6 percent per year, their contributed amount did not. As a result, most of my bank accounts were empty and I had two options: take out additional loans or try to make more money through scholarships or a side job. In order to make it through the year, I took out some emergency loans, which allowed me to attend school that year. I also began visiting the financial aid office weekly to try to come up with additional avenues for financial aid. Preferring to earn extra income rather than owe more money, I began to devise and follow through on a plan.

In order to pay for my education, I came up with the following options: transfer to UC (i.e. UCLA) or a state school in California, win a scholarship, or get a job that paid reasonably well. I did not spend much time considering transferring—I reasoned that I had decided to attend Harvey Mudd College so that I would not need to attend grad school to get a great job. Harvey Mudd provides hands-on, practical training with smaller class sizes; in addition, because Harvey Mudd has no graduate school, professors select undergraduates to be teaching assistants, tutors, and research assistants.

Winning a scholarship was the next option. I began researching scholarships on the internet and tried to find scholarships for which I actually qualified. It turned out to be difficult for a Caucasian male from an upper-middle-class family to find a financial need-based scholarship. Also, the opportunity to obtain a merit-based scholarship for college seemed to have passed. While I continued to search for scholarships that had were large enough relative to the effort required to apply for them and the low probability that I would win, I decided to work on my resume so that I could possibly earn a reasonable wage.

While I worked with the Career Services office on my resume and tried to land a paid summer internship, I decided to work on Plan B. I had earned decent money in high school by fixing and building computers. In order to get a job fixing computers at a reputable computer store, you need to be A+ certified, which requires studying from a 1,000-page book and passing an exam. Even though sophomore year is extremely difficult, I decided to work towards obtaining this certification. I eventually took and passed the exam and decided to move on to the Network+ certification, which was very complementary to my skills in computer repair and construction. At the same time, I worked as a computer lab assistant in order to get more Unix experience and pad my resume. In addition, I continued to work on the work study research project I had begun during the previous summer with a professor and another student.

In talking to fellow classmates about my financial problems, I found some students who had won a Microsoft Technical Scholarship that paid for tuition (everything but books, room, and board). Just like me, these students were Caucasian males. One student had written a 20,000-line chess program with AI (artificial intelligence) while still in high school, and was quite a prodigy; the other student was more like me—industrious, business-savvy, and well-rounded. I decided to apply for this scholarship, which required applicants to write four essays, obtain a letter of recommendation, and submit a resume along with an academic transcript. In addition to completing the application, applicants needed to go through the Microsoft internship interview process and be selected to work as a summer intern—which was very challenging. I had the opportunity to be interviewed on campus by a Microsoft recruiter, and eventually took a trip to Microsoft for the rigorous five- to seven-hour technical interview. While I waited to hear back from the scholarship committee and the Microsoft interview process, I continued to look for other opportunities.

While working in the computer lab one day, I saw an email sent to the CS department regarding a semester-long software development position, in which one student would join a group of three other students and a professor from the Claremont Graduate University. Without hesitation, I responded that I was interested in the position, attached my resume, and expressed my dire need to earn extra income. I was interviewed with a group of nine other students and was eventually selected. For this position, I had to commit to approximately 20 hours a week for the entire semester and produce a deliverable of a software library at the end of the term. The problem was that I had not met my teammates and determined whether they were up to the task; nor had I realized the implications of taking on this position with my current workload. Shortly after accepting the position, I learned that I had won the Microsoft Technical Scholarship and a summer internship at Microsoft, which meant that I would be able to pay for my junior year and at least a portion of my senior year. At this point, I quit the track team and began what turned out to be an extremely painful semester.

My work schedule was incredibly difficult. I would go to class, do homework, and work 15 hours a day so that I could work from noon on Friday to, on some occasions, 2 a.m. on Saturday morning in order to complete my work for the software development team. I would wake up early Saturday morning and work up until the team call to finish any remaining work. Even with this schedule, I was doing at least my portion of the work and meeting my deadlines. After a few weeks, it turned out that one team member was not pulling her weight and the rest of the team needed to pick up the slack. During this period, my grades suffered due to my lack of sleep, and I was barely able to complete my homework assignments. Even worse, because I had not made my setup ergonomic or discovered the computer athlete concept, I had numb and cold fingers, elbow and wrist pain, and tingling in my hand. Then I experienced one of the things that people encounter when they have one or more repetitive stress injuries; your body begins to feel strange; as a result, you have difficulty sleeping, which compounds the problem. During the week of midterms, I was in so much pain that I could not use the computer at all. I had developed trigger finger in my left index finger, among my other injuries, and was in a very bad situation.

After midterms, I had spring break and some time to recuperate. It was at this point that I faced the harsh reality that I would either need to find a profession that did not involve intense computer usage or fix my broken computer habits. I reasoned that it would be easier to fix my habits than to change my major, even though I was not sure whether I would recover or how long it would take. However, I did know that if I didn't fix my habits and recover, I would need to give up my Microsoft technical scholarship, internship, and two years of college tuition. Also, Computer Science was not something someone had pushed me into. I have had a passion for software and computers since I was 10, even though I had no mentors in the subject in my immediate family. As well, I still wanted to start my own software company one day. On a mission to fix my habits, I began to do research.

During my research, I read several books and visited numerous websites. I learned about proper keyboard height and desk height, the need to take breaks, stretching, and much more. During the course of my research, I stumbled across the phrase "computer athlete." Unfortunately, people were using the title of computer athlete to describe anyone who uses a computer more than a few hours a day. I asked myself "How could someone who is unhealthy, in pain, and using a computer incorrectly be a computer athlete?" On the other hand, when I thought of a computer athlete, I envisioned a person who was incredibly productive and happy using the computer. That vision was very different from the situation I found myself in; I was scared that my body would not heal itself from injury, angry at myself for over-committing, and in a lot of pain. From that point on, I began to develop my vision of the computer athlete, and began sharing this vision with my friends and family. I have spent thousands of hours developing, applying, and practicing the ideas that I am going to share with you. These ideas and principles can dramatically change your life.

During the week of my spring break, I stayed at school and worked on becoming a computer athlete, recuperating, and catching up on my work. I read three books and explored many online resources. I began to redesign my setup. I placed two-by-fours under my desk to raise it to the right height, bought a chair with lumbar support, and propped up my monitors on books. I bought a natural keyboard, a vertical mouse, and most importantly, a kinesis foot pedal. I configured the foot pedal to allow me to press Shift, Control, or Alt, or Control and Shift with one foot. The foot pedal allowed me to continue to use Emacs without forcing me to pronate or twist my hand in order to initiate commands or learn a new editor, as I was quite proficient at Emacs. I also started a strength and conditioning regimen, as well as an exercise regimen that would help me as a computer athlete. I made changes to my eating habits and reduced my consumption of caffeine. Meanwhile, I gradually increased my computer usage from 2 to four hours per day, taking long breaks between working sessions. By the end of the week, I was making small tweaks to my setup and was able to work a total of four hours on the computer per day. Through the rest of the semester, I continued to recuperate, minimized my computer usage, and made it through the semester with a decent GPA.

Through the semester, my pain gradually got better but did not go away. I still needed to make further changes. I knew the internship at Microsoft would be intense, so after the semester was over I learned the Dvorak keyboard layout, based on recommendations from my friends and the research I had done. Unlike QWERTY, the standard keyboard layout, Dvorak was designed with good ergonomics in mind. I pushed back my internship so that I had exactly two weeks before starting, giving me enough time to learn the new layout. I gradually became more adept at the new layout while still being able to use the old layout. Today, I am bi-layout. I can touch type in either layout, though I am much faster in Dvorak than I am in QWERTY.

The internship at Microsoft was extremely intense. I was working six days a week and ten hours a day, since I had a project that had a tight deadline. Microsoft has a sink-or-swim culture, and I was working in the Microsoft Office group, which is a cash cow of Microsoft. I continued to have pain, since I was pushing myself to the limit of my productivity using the tools I had and the computer athlete concept. I met my deadlines and some of my stretch goals and had a very successful internship at Microsoft.

When I came home from the internship, I had still more challenges to face. I had decided to play basketball with my uncle and my friend during my grandparents' anniversary party. While going for a rebound, the ball hit my finger, and I began to feel extreme pain. I continued to play for a few minutes and then decided that I could not play anymore; the pain had become too severe. I went to the Emergency Room and learned that my left index finger was broken. The timing was incredibly poor; I was going back to school in one week, and as a computer science major, I would need to use my hands to program.

With my left hand in a cast at the start of the semester, I was not off to a great start. To make matters worse, I was taking some rigorous programming courses, including Operating Systems, which required 30 hours of my time in one week at one point. By using the foot pedal, minimizing the typing that I needed to do, and using speech recognition with a Plantronics noise-filtering headset, I was able to complete my work for the semester. Fortunately, some of my programming courses allowed me to work with a partner, and I was able to focus more on design and code review as opposed to actually coding. Eventually, my hand healed and my two-year challenge with ergonomics in college ended.

During my senior year and for many years after college, I worked at a software startup company. As one of the first developers, technical specialists, and software architects at a startup company with a very small team, there was a lot of work to do, and my teammates and I had to wear many hats. For three years, I worked extremely hard. I worked more than ten hours a day, five to seven days a week to build the product-facing applications of our platform. The CEO of the company was surprised at my level of productivity and the hours of productivity I could output, both of which I attribute to being a computer athlete. During those years, I continued to have small aches and pains and made changes to my setup, equipment, and lifestyle to maintain pain-free computing and continue performing at my top level. As a result, I have dramatically improved my productivity and have developed and refined my concept of the computer athlete.

2. The Problem

Musculoskeletal pain affects you directly and indirectly. It can cause you pain and discomfort and dramatically decrease your quality of life. At its worst, it can lead you to pay expensive healthcare costs, force you to miss days at work, force you to change careers, or cause you debilitating injury. Indirectly, it can affect you by decreasing the productivity of your co-workers, family members, or the entire economy, and dramatically increase healthcare costs for everyone. These impacts offer further cause for concern, since the number of people who have access to a computer at home or work has and will increase steadily for the foreseeable future: as of the first quarter of 2008, the number of internet users in the world was over 1.3 billion out of the approximately 6.7 billion people in the world (Miniwatts Marketing Group, 2008). At the same time, the large-scale adoption of the internet and the personal computer is a relatively recent phenomenon. According to the U.S. Bureau of Labor Statistics, in 2003 computer-related injuries' direct and indirect costs were between $20 and $100 billion annually and affected millions of people in the U.S. alone. If people do not change their behavior, as the internet and computers increase in usage and scale, so too will the problem.

Unfortunately, there is no silver bullet for solving the problem of computer-related injury. In addition, the human body is complicated; there still quite a bit we don't understand about it. On the other hand, a number of contributing factors, or "bad apples," can be removed to generally improve the situation. Becoming a computer athlete ultimately means removing these known causes. What follows is not intended to be an exhaustive list of "bad apples," but at least it is a start.

First, we have poor standards and conventions when it comes to computer usage. For example, the standard convention for keyboard layouts is QWERTY, which stands for the order of the keys on the top row of the keyboard. However, other keyboard layouts have been developed, such as the Dvorak keyboard, patented in 1936, that have been shown to have significant ergonomic advantages over QWERTY. Yet people are still taught the QWERTY layout as beginners, and no other layout has received mainstream adoption. In addition, the standard mouse conventions exhibit poor ergonomics. Most mouses are intended to be used by laying your hand flat on top of them. This ambidextrous design allows you to use either your right or left hand to control the mouse, supporting both left- and right-handed people with a single design. Unfortunately, in order to accomplish this, you must twist your arm into an uncomfortable position while holding the mouse. In both of these cases, technology is not the issue. Other layouts and more ergonomic mouse and keyboard designs and products have existed for years, but individual

users and the industry have failed to adopt them.
Essentially, this is an adoption and education problem.

Poor, antiquated industry standards and conventions are
used for interfacing with a computer.

Second, individuals, either because they are under
pressure from their employers or due to personal drive,
exceed their body's limitations. Imagine that you are taking
a tiny hammer and hitting it against the small joints in your
hands for several hours a day. Your body can heal itself
when you sleep and receive proper nourishment, but after
too many days spending long hours playing an instrument,
using a computer, or performing some other repetitive
activity, the damage you cause will exceed your body's
ability to heal itself. You need to understand your body's
limits and not exceed them.

People work past their body's ability to repair itself.

Third, when people experience pain from using a
computer, more often than not they take no action—or they
take the wrong action. Typically, debilitating injury from
using a computer does not happen in a single day. Rather,
these injuries are developed over a long period of time, as
individuals experience pain and fail to resolve it. There are
warning signs: numbness, cold fingers, sharp pain,
difficulty sleeping, and so on. If people could simply learn
to change their habits and work environment when they
experience these symptoms, computer-related injury could
be much less of a problem.

More often than not, people fail either to make changes or make the right types of changes to fix the root cause of their problem.

The twentieth-century smallpox epidemic and its subsequent virtual eradication offer an example of the type of response that leads to a solution. During the twentieth century, smallpox was responsible for 300-500 million deaths (Wikipedia, 2010). After the smallpox vaccine was developed, the disease was eradicated through the efforts of the World Health Organization (WHO) led in part by Dr. Larry Brilliant, who applied the strategy of "early detection and rapid response." The pain of computer-related injuries could be similarly eradicated through early detection and rapid and appropriate response. In many cases today, individuals respond either too slowly or incorrectly. For instance, people tend to visit their primary care physician when they experience musculoskeletal pain caused by their computer usage. Because your doctor does not have control of or visibility into your personal decisions, work habits, or work environment, he or she may not be able to solve the root cause of your pain. In order to deal with this issue, people need to be more proactive, or at least reactive, to their pain and seek the appropriate response. In fact, with only a basic understanding of ergonomics and the computer athlete model, you can quickly determine changes that will help improve your situation. A large-scale media campaign and focused grassroots efforts could help tackle this issue of computer-related injuries.

Unfortunately, today, computers are predominantly controlled mechanically: you have to push buttons on a keyboard or move a mouse in order to control your computer, a situation that sets the stage for repetitive stress injuries. In the future, computer-user interfacing may not be limited by the need for mechanical operation; personally, I am very optimistic that technology will help mitigate the problem over time. However, it seems that each new technology comes with its own problems and tradeoffs. In the short term, we need to reinforce proper training regarding ergonomics and health when learning to use a computer.

Many types of injuries can result from computer use: neck or back pain, tendonitis, trigger finger, carpal tunnel, and thoracic outlet syndrome are just a few examples. Depending on your profession and how you use your computer, you could be at risk for developing one of these injuries. People in numerous professional fields are at risk: software developers, graphics designers, website developers, students, writers, investment bankers, lawyers— any profession that requires the use of a computer. If you have reason to believe that you have or are developing one of these injuries, seek the right assistance as early as possible.

If we can solve or reduce the prevalence of this problem, there will be many benefits. First, people will be more productive, as they will be able to focus on what they are trying to accomplish instead of on their pain. Second, resources currently allocated to treating injuries could be used for other purposes; according to the National Institute of Neurological Disorders and Stroke (NINDS), the direct lifetime cost of carpal tunnel is estimated at $30,000. Finally, and perhaps most importantly, a person's quality of life will drastically improve if he or she does not experience pain while using the computer—an activity that may constitute a large portion of a person's life. In total, most knowledge workers probably spend over one-third of their lives on the computer, which amounts to most of their waking hours.

The rest of this book focuses on how individuals can help solve this problem by learning the principles of a computer athlete.

3. Orientation

Imagine that you wake up on Monday morning refreshed from your previous night's sleep and excited to start your week. You eat a hearty breakfast, put a lunch together, and head off to work. You are alert and feel good, even without energy drinks or coffee. As you progress through the day, you stay hydrated and nourished as you complete your tasks and objectives. At work, you tackle issues as they arise and make solid progress. Eventually, your day ends and you head home. When home, you complete your chores, perhaps exercise, eat dinner, and spend the remainder of the night either with your family or enjoying some leisure time. Then, you prepare for the next day and go to sleep early enough to ensure that you will get enough sleep for the next day. When you are using the computer, you are focused, alert, and happily working away. You gently press the keys, gracefully use the mouse, and your body is relaxed and in a neutral position. Now, compare that vision to your current situation. How closely does your current lifestyle mirror this vision?

This apparently idealized existence characterizes the experience of a computer athlete. Such an existence is not only achievable, but necessary if you intend to continue working on a computer for many years to come. As you spend more time on the computer, it becomes more important to be a computer athlete; for example, the more hours you spend typing, the more important it is to have a keyboard with low keyboard pressure to minimize the wear and tear on your joints. Your quality of life cannot be high if it is filled with dread at going to work, concern over your physical well-being, and physical and mental pain. Fortunately, all of that is avoidable. *You* are in control of how you use your computer, the keyboard layout you use, how you react to stress, what and when you eat, and how much sleep you get.

You don't need to make dramatic changes all at once. You can gradually change your habits and work environment until you reach a state of pain-free computing. One in three people who use a computer regularly experience some pain while using it. You can help reduce that statistic. Be pro-active.

The rest of this book describes the types of changes you can make in order to become a computer athlete. You can learn from the experience of others and avoid making the same mistakes. You can read the chapters out of order, since they are independent of each other. The five areas of mastery (Equipment and Usage, Nutrition, Self-Care & Self-Awareness, Strength and Conditioning, and Stress Management) are meant to be worked on simultaneously. Try to make some changes in each of these areas on a weekly or monthly basis until you find that your computing is pain-free. You may need assistance in making these changes—so ask for help and use your resources. You can search and connect with people on the internet, research ergonomic products, or work together with someone with similar goals. Keep in mind that the hard work is on the front end. Once you establish good habits, it is relatively easy to maintain them. That work will pay dividends over time, especially if you spend a large portion of your life working at the computer.

Finally, a warning: when it comes to ergonomics, ignorance is not bliss. Ignorance can be the cause of debilitating injury and pain. Once you are armed with the knowledge of how to fix your habits and work environment, you will be compelled to change them, because you should never do anything dumb on purpose. It's one thing to do dumb things by accident, but in general it's a good life rule to minimize the number of dumb things you do. Once you know that your computer habits are hurting your body and undermining your quality of life, why would you continue down the same road?

The Computer Athlete's Handbook

4. Equipment and Usage

A computer athlete has the right equipment—and also uses it properly. You can purchase the right equipment and have a great setup, but still develop debilitating injuries through improper use. For example, I have seen people who had two monitors but placed one monitor off to the side so that they had to twist their neck in order to see the screen. As a result, they developed pain in their neck and back.

Just as with proper usage, using proper equipment is also incredibly important. If a small-framed computer athlete uses a keyboard that requires a large amount of pressure to press and hold the keys relative to their strength and body size, it is likely that the repetitive stress of typing will lead to injury. Pushing down on the keys becomes akin to taking a tiny hammer and hitting one's fingers thousands of times a day. Doing something that causes a small amount of wear and tear a few times can lead to a small problem. Doing something that causes a small amount of pain a large number of times, however, can lead to a big problem. Use of the wrong keyboard for your body can cause extreme hand and finger pain.

A computer athlete has the right equipment and uses it properly.

The "right" equipment will vary based on the computer athlete's body frame and workload. This fact should not be surprising, since athletes customize their equipment all the time. Track & field athletes, for example, purchase shoes that fit their foot length and width and will best support their feet for the type of running they will be doing. Some runners purchase additional equipment, called orthotics, to give additional support to the arch of their foot.

By contrast, most computers users use a standard mouse and keyboard that does not meet their needs or workload. Why? Is it that people are unaware that other options are available? Ergonomic computer equipment isn't advertised through mainstream media channels (TV, radio, print) yet. Is it that people or companies do not want to pay the upfront cost of purchasing the right hardware? It can easily be shown that purchasing the right equipment will increase productivity and offer a great return on the investment. Both the marketing void and companies' stinginess are problems that may be on the way out, since market pressure will probably have its usual effect: now that people are starting to use computers by the age of 5, the need for equipment that varies by body frame will only increase. Imagine going to the store to buy a tiny keyboard for your child, just as you would buy tiny shoes for a toddler.

Brian Bentow

Fortunately, great equipment is already out there: many companies already manufacture ergonomic computer equipment, and there is even a National Ergonomics Conference and Exposition held annually where vendors demonstrate their products and services. Many great keyboards, mouses, and alternate input devices exist and can be found easily on the internet. I will discuss some of these devices. Although the devices will change over time, the principles involved will probably remain the same.

The best equipment for each computer athlete will vary based on his or her body style and workload.

A computer athlete obtains and uses input devices based on sound ergonomic principles. The devices may include a keyboard, mouse, and alternate input devices (foot pedals, foot mouse, voice recognition, etc).

Keyboards

For many computer users, the keyboard is their most important input device. Unfortunately, the keyboard is an often-misused tool. Every key that you press makes an impact on your body; keyboard use is a highly mechanical process. The goal is to minimize this impact while maintaining your productivity so that you can be productive for longer periods of time.

A computer athlete minimizes the impacts caused by using input devices.

You can minimize this impact in a number of ways. The easiest of these techniques is to purchase a low-impact keyboard. The impact caused by everyday use of the keyboard stems from numerous factors, many of which can be improved quite easily. The amount of force required to press a key and the distance your fingers need to travel, as well as how the keys behave once they have been pressed, are all important factors in minimizing impact. If you determine that you need a new keyboard, don't let the daunting number of options prevent you from realizing at least some improvement. You may even need to try a keyboard out for several weeks or months before you know if it is the right one. Since you use a keyboard every day, it makes sense to invest the time and money to find the right one for you.

All keyboards are not created equal.

Many ergonomic challenges come along with working on a laptop, and more and more people face these challenges as the number of laptop computers sold exceeds the number of desktop computers sold. First of all, a laptop keyboard and monitor are very close together. Ideally, the keyboard should be close to your body so that you don't have to reach for it, whereas the monitor should be at a full arm's distance away. Second, because space is limited, laptop keys tend to be closer together, which can be uncomfortable for people who need a split keyboard. Third, the keys tend to be flat; as a result, when typing on a laptop, you may find yourself resting your wrists on a surface. Due to these intrinsic challenges, there are limits to how ergonomic a laptop keyboard can be. I recommend either using an external keyboard or selecting a laptop with a keyboard that does a good job of meeting your ergonomic needs and minimizing the amount of typing you do away from your more ergonomic setup.

Laptop users face many challenges.

There are many keyboard styles, some of which are quite exotic. The objective is to find a keyboard that allows you to keep your shoulder, arm, and wrist in a comfortable, neutral position. A standard keyboard layout places all the keys in one contiguous region. Unlike a natural keyboard (such as the Microsoft Natural Keyboard), a standard keyboard has no split in the center. For people with narrow shoulders, the fact that this keyboard lacks a separation between the left and right side may not be problematic. A narrow-framed user may be able to have his or her shoulders in a neutral position and reach for the keys without having to pronate their wrists or push their arms together. In addition, many standard keyboards take up less space, allowing the user to keep his or her mouse in closer proximity. For narrow-shouldered people, I recommend looking for a standard keyboard that is wide enough for them to maintain a neutral position.

A computer athlete uses input devices that enable him to maintain neutral positions.

For broader-framed people, however, a standard keyboard can be incredibly uncomfortable. The next option is to purchase a split or natural keyboard that either has a fixed angled of separation or allows you to vary the angle of separation. The split design allows you to keep your arm and wrist in a neutral position while typing. Although split keyboards encourage natural wrist and arm alignment, they can force you to place your shoulders in a non-neutral position. For this reason, it is important to find a keyboard that has enough flexibility to allow you to adjust the left and right sides so that each arm, wrist, and shoulder can be in a neutral position. One of the keyboards I purchased was a 2006 award recipient at the Natural Ergonomics Expo called the Kinesis FreeStyle. It allows you to separate the left and right side up to 20 inches and can be split at the center by varying degrees, as well as angled vertically using accessories. It helped me eliminate the pain I had in my chest muscles caused by using a Natural Keyboard. There is no one-size-fits-all keyboard. Just as a runner must find the right pair of sneakers, a computer athlete must find the right keyboard to meet his or her needs.

The width of your shoulders and the size of your frame will impact your search for a keyboard that allows you to keep your body in neutral positions.

Once you have obtained a keyboard that is aligned with your physical dimensions, you can focus on improving your usage patterns. When building a house, you need to use the right tool for the job. When using a keyboard, it is important to rely on larger fingers to carry heavier workloads. The pinky finger is the smallest digit and was not designed to do "heavy lifting" on the keyboard. The ring or fourth finger and the third or middle fingers are more robust, and should be used where possible to maximize productivity and reduce stress on the pinky and index finger. For example, rather than press the arrow, Control, and Shift keys with more fragile digits, you can move your entire hand and push these keys with your third and/or fourth finger. A colleague of mine developed trigger finger in his right pinky from overusing his pinky to press the arrow keys. It was incredibly painful, and prevented him from using his pinky again for several weeks. Notice how you type and press commands on your keyboard and try to optimize the fingers you use. It is best to change your usage patterns *before* you develop pain.

Use larger appendages, where possible, to handle heavier workloads and increase productivity.

In addition to using the wrong fingers to press certain keys, a common mistake computer users make is to pronate, or twist, the hand in order to reach for multiple keys with a single hand. For example, it is common for people to create the symbol "A" by pressing Shift and "a" with their left hand. In order to press the key combination with one hand, you must twist your hand, which can cause carpal tunnel or other wrist problems. To prevent pronation and its associated problems, press Shift with your right hand and the "a" key with your left hand.

Avoid pronation, or twisting your wrist to press multiple keys at one time.

Another way to eliminate pronating your hand and to leverage larger appendages where possible is to use an alternate input device (i.e. a foot pedal) and to press keys using your feet. I will discuss foot pedals later on—they are incredibly valuable tools for increasing productivity.

Another common pitfall is that computer users, attempting to be more productive, increase the work and impact they incur on their bodies with no real gain in productivity. When we envision a computer athlete, we see a person who works gracefully and deftly. Whether from stress, habit, or a lack of tactile acuity, some users hammer down on the keys, placing unnecessary stress on fragile fingers. In general, one should not try to type as fast as possible or use excessive force when typing.

A computer athlete gracefully completes his tasks without using excessive force or keystrokes.

In addition, in trying to increase productivity, some users switch rapidly between applications when they are running several applications at the same time. After a certain point, this switching adds no increase in productivity, but simply tires you out and distracts you. Be aware of your usage patterns, and try to avoid using excessive force or keystrokes to accomplish a task that requires much less effort.

A useful tool for eliminating repetitive keystrokes is a Macro—a recorded set of keystrokes that can be replayed on command. A number of applications support Macros, including Vi, Emacs, Microsoft Word 2007, TextPad, and others. You can create a body of text, paste it into a program that supports Macros, record and apply a Macro a number of times, and then paste the final text wherever you need it. If you find yourself performing a repetitive set of keystrokes on a list of items, a Macro can not only eliminate keystrokes but also dramatically increase productivity. For example, you can run a Macro many times within a fraction of a second, enabling you to complete a task in minutes that would otherwise have taken hours.

In order to eliminate keystrokes, a computer athlete employs the tools at his disposal.

Due to the strenuous nature of using a computer, computer athletes should not overwork themselves. In order to reduce wear and tear, a computer athlete takes breaks and avoids unnecessary computer usage—for example, by eliminating excessive instant messaging and emailing when a phone call is possible. Instant messaging offers many benefits, including having a transcript of the conversation and being cost-free. The problem is, because we can talk much faster than we can type and tend to want to instant message conversationally, instant messaging can cause excessively fast typing and lead to increased wear and tear.

A computer athlete avoids overuse.

Keyboard Layouts

Keyboard layout significantly impacts typist fatigue. The standard keyboard layout has the keys Q-W-E-R-T-Y on the top row and is therefore referred to as QWERTY. The QWERTY layout appeared on the first commercially successful typewriter, invented by Christopher Sholes in the 1860s. It was designed to avoid key jams by causing successive keystrokes to occur on alternating sides of the keyboard. Unfortunately, this layout increased typist fatigue and slowed down typing. Even more unfortunately, despite advances made in keyboards and typewriters since the 19th century that have rendered the QWERTY layout unnecessary, no layout has yet displaced QWERTY as the standard keyboard layout.

Using an ergonomic keyboard layout can lead to dramatic increases in comfort and productivity.

There are options, however. In the 1930s, a new layout called Dvorak (named for its inventor, Dr. August Dvorak) was developed, based on sound ergonomic principles. His layout was designed to the following specifications:

1. The most common letters and digraphs should be the easiest to type. For example, on a Dvorak keyboard, the vowels and major consonants are on the home row.

2. The least common letters should be the hardest to type—on the bottom row.

3. The right hand should do most of the typing, because most people are right-handed.

4. Letters should be placed in a way that encourages inboard stroke flow, meaning that keystrokes start from the outside of the keyboard and move inward.

I wrote this book using the Dvorak layout, which is popular among computer programmers. It's also popular among the super-speedy: since 1985, Dvorak layout user Barbara Blackburn has held the record for typing at 150 wpm (words per minute), according to the Guinness Book of World Records. Off the record, she has been measured to type at the staggering pace of 212 wpm. Dvorak not only decreases the distance your fingers need to travel, but has also been demonstrated to improve typing accuracy, increasing productivity and decreasing wear and tear because errors and corrections are made less frequently.

My purpose in discussing the Dvorak layout is not to recommend that every computer athlete learn an entirely new typing layout based on its benefits. Instead, I believe that it inspires us to challenge the conventional standard, realizing that initial standards can be extremely difficult to overcome. Another example of this phenomenon can be found in the fact that the United States, Liberia, and Burma (Myanmar) are the only countries left that use the English system of measurement as their official standard. Even England has officially chosen the metric system over the English system! In the 1970s, a large group of stakeholders from the public and private sectors in the U.S. deliberated and determined that it would be best for the U.S. to move officially over to the metric system, as well. However, as of 2008, the U.S. still, inexplicably, uses the English system. One could similarly argue that the QWERTY standard should be replaced as the de facto keyboard standard, since several superior keyboard layouts exist— including Colemak, Dvorak, and the like.

Although learning another layout can take several weeks and make using keyboards on QWERTY workstations more difficult, it can be worth the effort. If you spend the majority of your time on your own workstation, the fact that using other workstations could be more difficult may not affect you significantly. It is also possible to be bi-layout. I know both QWERTY and Dvorak well, and can switch between them when necessary. I will say, though, that while I am pretty adept at Dvorak, my QWERTY typing has suffered a bit.

Overall, typing on a more ergonomic layout is more comfortable and reduces fatigue, so if you spend a sufficiently large amount of time on the computer, the investment of time makes a lot of sense. I encourage computer programmers, secretaries, or anyone who is required to use the keyboard for long periods of time on a regular basis to learn about alternate keyboard layouts. A computer athlete would focus on learning a new layout if he/she had used other techniques to increase comfort and wanted that extra boost. Most modern operating systems let you change the keyboard layout pretty easily; you can even use a keyboard that has QWERTY labeled keys and just type in your new layout. In fact, I have not relabeled my keys and use a keyboard with QWERTY labeled keys to this day. However, I recommend that most people purchase a re-lettering kit and re-label their keys, which will make it easier to learn the new layout.

Several other layouts besides Dvorak merit attention. Colemak supposedly has many of the benefits of

Dvorak, but is easier to learn. Colemak was released in 2006, and is quite new relative to Dvorak and QWERTY.

Mouses

Selecting the right mouse can be incredibly important—nearly as important as selecting a keyboard.

The standard mouse design is another legacy from the earliest days of computing. The mouse was invented by Douglas Engelbart in 1963; in 1972, Bill English invented the ball mouse while working for Xerox PARC. Over time, new versions of mechanical and, later, optical mouses were developed. Even as advances were made in tracking technology, the standard design, in which the mouse's buttons are located on the top of the mouse (requiring you to twist your arm in order to use it), has remained relatively unchanged. One benefit to having the mouse buttons on the top of the mouse as opposed to on the left or right side is that you can use the mouse whether you are left or right-handed. This design, however, leads to discomfort and injury.

Be extremely careful how you use your mouse; it is a common cause of injury.

The standard mouse isn't your only option; other mouses are more comfortable and ergonomic. For example, there is a vertical mouse made by Evoluent that enables you to mouse without having to twist your hand. The buttons are on the right hand side for a right-handed mouse and on the left-hand side for a left-handed mouse. This set-up brings considerable comfort to people who mouse frequently, such as graphic designers. I have used a vertical mouse and found it to be much more comfortable than a standard mouse. For computer users with relatively small hands, there is a type of computer mouse that looks like a joystick and can be used as a vertical mouse.

Just as the way you hold the mouse is important, the mouse's movement sensitivity can have a significant impact. If your mouse is too sensitive, you will need to tense your small muscles in order to move it accurately. This phenomenon is similar to the fatigue surgeons experience when they have to move their fingers very precisely. Conversely, by using a less sensitive mouse and moving it with your arm and shoulder, you can allow a larger muscle group to perform most of the work. This strategy is aligned with the principle of using larger body parts or muscle groups to handle heavier workloads. For this reason, I am not a fan of trackball mouses, because they require you to use your fingers as opposed to your shoulder to do most of the work.

Another common cause of pain is mouse clicking. If you need to perform a significant amount of mouse clicking, you may want to consider using an alternate input device, like a foot pedal, so that you can click using your foot. The amount of force needed to click the mouse can produce wear and tear just as keyboard key pressure can. It is important to find a mouse with a comfortable button click and to find ways to use large muscle groups to assist in your mousing.

Consider alternate input devices in order to increase productivity and minimize impact to smaller body parts.

Alternate Input Devices

While using the computer, your feet and legs are typically idle. Such a set-up is pretty wasteful, since your legs are your larger appendages and, as discussed before, it's better to use larger appendages to do more of the work. In order to use your legs and feet to assist in your computing, you can use a foot pedal, foot switch, or foot mouse. Foot pedals come in a variety of "flavors" and usually have 1-4 programmable buttons. Typically, people program these buttons to perform left and right mouse-clicks or to press common keys like Shift and Control. By pressing Control and/or Shift with your foot, you can avoid pronating your hand and increase your productivity. For example, to press "A," you can press Shift with your foot and the "a" key with your hand. In the keyboard section, we discussed how to avoid pronating your hand by shifting your hand position and pressing Shift with your third and fourth fingers. However, by using an alternate input device, you can avoid this hand movement and potential productivity loss entirely.

Foot pedals are commonly used in flight simulator games or when gamers want to increase their speed. Whatever the reason, purchasing a foot pedal can be a great investment. A foot mouse typically has one foot for cursor control and another foot for mouse clicking. Learning to use a foot pedal or foot mouse may take several days to get used to. However, the benefit makes it worth the effort.

Voice Recognition

Voice recognition involves the conversion of audible speech to text or to commands to instruct a computer program. It has been used in IVR (interactive voice recognition) systems such as a company phone directory, phone customer service, and dictation software. Anyone who has used voice recognition knows that it is not perfect. The software must overcome different accents, speech patterns, background noise, and many other challenges. It also has many limitations, some of which are intrinsic to its nature. First, most people are unable to use voice recognition at work, either because talking to their computer would distract their co-workers or because the voice recognition software would pick up other people's speech. Secondly, if you have ever tried talking for even a few hours, you have probably noted that your vocal cords become tired. Using voice recognition for long periods of time would probably have the same effect. Finally, depending on what your goals are, the value that you receive from using voice recognition may not justify using it. For example, if you find that you have to spend a significant amount of time correcting mistakes after using voice recognition, it may not make sense to use it. That being said, my own personal experience and from other anecdotal evidence shows that using voice recognition can still be a viable alternative to typing.

Setup and Posture

The setup of your work environment is intrinsically linked to your posture. If you have a bad setup, you will have bad posture. For instance, if your computer screen is too far away from you, you may hunch forward to read the screen. If your screen is too high, too low, or off center, you will need to bend your neck in an awkward position. The good news is that you can avoid many pitfalls and problems by setting up your workstation properly.

When setting up your workstation, the goal is to allow your body parts to remain in a neutral position. The neutral position for a particular body part is the correct ergonomic position that reduces stress and fatigue on your muscles and joints. For most body parts, it is very obvious how to achieve the neutral position.

Set up your workstation so that your body parts can be positioned neutrally.

For example, your elbow's neutral position is bent at 90 degrees. A common pitfall is placing your keyboard or mouse on a surface that is too high to let your elbow be at 90 degrees. In general, you will need to place your keyboard on your lap, adjust your table height or chair height, or use an adjustable keyboard tray. Personally, I place my keyboard on my lap, because such positioning does not require purchasing any additional equipment and can be done whether I am at home or working at another location.

The neutral position for your elbow is bent at 90 degrees.

Next, the neutral position for your wrists is straight, bent neither to the left nor the right. Attaining a neutral wrist position will vary based on your shoulder width and frame. For example, small-framed or narrow people may be able to use a standard flat keyboard or a laptop keyboard. On the other hand, wider people may need to use a natural keyboard that is split or an adjustable split keyboard so that their wrists can remain in a neutral position. You can look at your wrists and arms while you type to determine whether your wrists are straight and at a neutral position.

Use a keyboard that allows you to keep your wrists straight and in a neutral position.

Another pitfall is positioning the mouse too far from your body. The neutral position for your shoulder is relaxed. Raising your arm is tiring and will lead to shoulder and neck pain. The goal is to be able to use your mouse so that your elbow is at 90 degrees and your shoulder muscle is relaxed. To accomplish this, you can purchase a keyboard/mouse tray, adjust the height of your chair or desk, or put a chair next to you and stack some books on it.

Keep your mouse close to your body and at the right height in order to remain at a neutral position.

When I am on the road, I create a makeshift desk by putting a chair with no arms and a flat seat as close to me as possible. Then I stack several books, a mouse pad, and my mouse on top of the seat. I adjust the stack of books until I can mouse with my shoulder and elbow in a neutral position without having to reach for my mouse. I have been able to replicate this process in many different locations and have shown several people how to do it as well.

Keeping your shoulders in a neutral position has been overlooked by many keyboard manufacturers. Even most natural keyboards are not split widely enough for most people. You may develop chest, back, or shoulder pain if your keyboard is too narrow. Personally, I use a tethered Kinesis FreeStyle, placing one side of the keyboard on each side of my lap. It would be best to have an adjustable keyboard tray, but once again, you can take your lap wherever you go, which is not necessarily true for the keyboard tray.

In general, you want to keep your feet flat on the floor, as this keeps your weight centered over your body. Some people like to cross their legs in their chair or sit on their leg. Unfortunately, these positions will tweak your spine and are not ideal postures. If you are too short, you should buy a foot rest so that your feet can rest flat on it. When using a foot pedal, resting your feet on a flat surface can be more difficult. This is why I prefer Frag Petals, as they can be pushed with your big toe with relatively little force. You can also activate the button while keeping your foot mostly flat.

Keep your feet flat on the floor.

Not surprisingly, you should avoid sitting up straight in a rigid position all day. Move around! At the very least, you can periodically lean forward for 30 seconds and then lean backwards. I also look up, down, or to the side periodically when I do not necessarily need to look at the screen.

Do not try to remain upright in a rigid position all day.

Your wrists and hands should be positioned so that your fingers drop down comfortably on the keys. If your keyboard is at the right height, this position occurs naturally. It is important not to rest your wrists on any hard surface. In general, I recommend refraining from using gel pads or arm rests, as resting your wrist on any surface will generate friction and heat and is somewhat of a crutch. With proper strength and conditioning and the use neutral positions, you should not need to rely on armrests, wrist braces, or any other support mechanism.

You can avoid the need for armrests or wrist rests with proper strength and conditioning and by using neutral positions.

Finally, finding the ergonomic, neutral position for your back can be difficult. Most people spend most of their lives sitting. They sit at work, at the movies, while eating, and while driving. Unfortunately, sitting puts a lot of pressure on your lower back. The conventional wisdom is to use a comfortable chair with good armrests and lumbar support. Once again, conventional wisdom may be wrong. Instead, many believe that you should try to engage in autonomous sitting where you do not rest your arms or back on any surface. You can achieve this by building strength and endurance in your lower back and core.

Sitting in a chair improperly is a leading cause of back pain.

Using neutral positions, a computer athlete can work at a computer without pain or fatigue for many hours. Attaining these positions is not difficult; it is, in fact, much easier and requires less effort than other positions. Yet surprisingly, most people struggle and maintain difficult and uncomfortable positions all day long.

Usage Patterns

It is important that you understand how you use the computer so that you can focus on your problem areas. An incredible amount of variation exists among different types of users. A writer may spend a large amount of time reading and editing, whereas an investment analyst may spend a great deal of time working in Excel, pressing the Control and various function keys. Depending on your usage and job function, you may benefit from making certain changes more than others.

Like a mechanic working on a car, you need to pick the right tool for the job. All keyboards, mouses, and other input devices are not created equal. If you are a graphic designer, you should use something other than a standard mouse. Similarly, if you are a programmer or a writer, you may want to consider using a low-force keyboard or a non-QWERTY layout. There are other tools besides input devices that you can leverage.

To get the most value, you should keep an open mind, think about your usage, and pick the techniques described in this book that can help you attain pain-free computing.

Bringing it all Together

Here are some prioritized changes you can make to your setup in order to compute in comfort. These prices are from 2008 and will vary; I mention them simply for illustrative purposes.

1. Under-desk Keyboard Tray - $100 to $200

2. Additional Monitor for Dual VGA (depends on video card support) - $100 to $300

3. Chair - $100 to $300

4. Keyboard - $30 to $200 and roughly 1 to 2 days' retraining

5. Mouse - $30 - $100 and 1 to 4 hours' retraining

6. Alternate Input Device - $100 to $400 and 1 to 2 days' retraining

7. Voice Recognition - $100 to $900 and 1to 4 weeks' retraining

8. Alternate Keyboard Layout - $0 and 1 to 3 weeks' retraining

These suggestions have been ordered to minimize cost and maximize your return on investment. The above is not intended to be an all-encompassing list. Your usage patterns and needs will affect your priorities as you purchase these items.

5. Nutrition

A computer athlete, like any athlete, needs quality nutrition in order to perform. Everyone has different needs as far as calories are concerned, and some have particular dietary restrictions, as well. But the focus here is on satisfying your own personal needs. Envision a computer athlete eating fresh fruit, protein or supplement bars, and whole foods, and drinking from a water bottle that is filled with fresh, filtered water. Then compare that with the stereotype of a computer programmer—aka a "code monkey." A code monkey consumes large amounts of soda; Mountain Dew is his favorite beverage. His favorite food is pizza. It is often said that if you need programmers to work through the night, you should give them Red Bull, Mountain Dew, and pizza. Although it is true that the brain and nervous system rely on glucose to function, long-term consumption of large amounts of soda and pizza will lead to very serious health problems.

While many professionals rely on coffee and soda to get through the day, I believe that caffeine should be avoided. Caffeine is a stimulant and causes you to urinate more frequently, which can lead to dehydration. When you are dehydrated and working at the computer, you are more susceptible to computer-related injury, because the body needs to be well-hydrated to support normal bodily function and repair itself. On top of that, as a stimulant, caffeine lets you work past your normal threshold, past the point where you would normally take a break. You can see that the combination of caffeine's stimulating and dehydrating effects can definitely contribute to developing an injury.

Becoming a computer athlete may require you to avoid consuming certain foods and the side effects that come with them.

I admit that the notion of avoiding caffeine is novel. Coffee and espresso consumption is so widely socially accepted that most people don't challenge its necessity. I believe that breaking one's dependence on caffeine requires dispelling the myth that people need caffeine to be productive. When I was in high school, I was concerned that I would have to start drinking coffee and soda in college in order to complete my studies. When I mentioned this to one of my uncles, who is a dentist, he told me that he made it through his undergraduate years and dental school and did quite well without drinking coffee or large amounts of caffeine from any source. From this anecdotal evidence, I learned that it was possible not to consume caffeine and still to do well in school and work. For my own part, I completed most of my undergraduate studies and worked for a startup company for several years without consuming caffeine. I even worked in Seattle for two summers, where Starbucks and Seattle's Best are extremely popular, without drinking coffee! Besides avoiding becoming dehydrated, I have also saved money and avoided damaging or staining my teeth. It is also important to note that I get a solid eight hours of sleep at night, eat well, exercise, and stay relatively fit. I am still able to be alert and productive at work. In fact, I am more alert and productive than my counterparts.

In order to stay hydrated, it is also important to keep water near your workstation. Having to get up and get a drink frequently will reduce your productivity and most likely lead to drinking less water than you should. Instead, you should keep water within arm's distance so that you can drink water throughout the day. You can grab a sip of water as you ponder or take one of the many short breaks you should be taking while working.

Just as crucial as keeping water nearby is keeping healthy snacks convenient. The average person who is hungry and has a bag of chips within arm's reach will eat those chips; however, if you have only healthy snacks nearby, you will find yourself eating healthy snacks when hungry—so make sure to stock up on nutritious munchies. Because your brain needs glucose to function, eating food throughout the day will keep your brain in prime working order.

The need to eat regularly leads to the next code monkey stereotype. Most computer programmers are either emaciated and sickly or quite overweight. I believe that these two unhealthy variations stem from differences in metabolism and eating habits, and manifest the way that different body types behave when subjected to a sedentary lifestyle. Fortunately, there has been a trend toward improving the quality of the food near computer programmers as employers have noticed their employees' health deteriorating.

A computer athlete establishes good eating habits and meal timing for optimal productivity and health.

At Microsoft, where I interned in the summer of 2003 and 2004, healthier eating was trendy. For many years, Microsoft employees had been elated that they were provided with free soda, Gatorade, and juice. Then, probably as a result of increasing health issues and movies like *Super-Size Me* entering into the mainstream media, Microsoft began adding low-sugar alternatives like seltzer, water, and milk to their free drink repertoire.

Some programmers I have met have had serious health issues. From sitting at the computer all day, they have developed large fat deposits on their back, on their thighs, or around their mid-sections. These fat deposits are sometimes exaggerated and disproportionate to the rest of their bodies. Most people are astonished when they hear of or see someone with one of these more advanced health issues.

I would guess that the number of programmers with health problems like diabetes is disproportionately high. The loss of productivity and cost caused by programmers' poor eating and exercise habits should motivate the company to facilitate and offer incentives for healthier choices.

The bottom line is that in order to set yourself up for success, you must establish good habits. Purchase healthy snacks and make sure to keep them nearby, whether you are at work or at home. Also, keep water nearby. Try to avoid eating a large lunch, which will put you in what I call a "food coma" and make you sleepy. Make an effort to prepare your own lunch, so you can be certain of what you are putting into your body and ensure that you are satisfying your nutritional needs.

For illustrative purposes, I will detail what I consume on an average day as a 6-foot-tall, 180-pound mesomorph (athletically built) programmer:

Until 7:10 am - Sleep

7:10 am – 8:00 am

1. Whole grain cereal

8:00 am – 10:00 am

1. Banana
2. Organic low-fat yogurt

11:00 am – 1 pm

1. Hard-boiled egg
2. Bagel with cream cheese

1 pm – 2 pm

1. Turkey sandwich on whole grain bread

2 pm – 5 pm

1. Protein bar
2. Whole grain granola bar
3. Crackers

6 pm – 8 pm

1. Dinner : salad + main course

8 pm – 10 pm

1. Fruit
2. Small dessert

11 pm - Sleep

As you can see, I don't have a large lunch. Instead, I consume small meals throughout the day. By the time dinner rolls around, I am hungry but not ravenous. I typically consume a moderate dinner and a small dessert meal.

6. Self-Awareness and Self-Care

Self-awareness is a heightened perception of your thoughts, actions, and perceptions, while self-care is the act of making decisions and taking actions that promote your health and well-being.

To become a computer athlete, you must be self-aware so that you can identify what aspects of your environment and work habits can be improved to minimize pain and discomfort. Then you must make changes, tuning your environment and work habits to make progress toward a state of pain-free computing. The actual changes you will need to make for pain-free computing will be unique to you; every computer athlete requires a slightly different regimen. Fortunately, self-awareness can help you determine which changes you will need to make. Self-awareness can be as simple as noticing that you are experiencing pain or discomfort somewhere in your body. Developing self-awareness will enable you to design your ideal work environment based on your individual needs.

Once you determine what actions you need to take, it's time to follow through and execute them. At this point, self-care enters the picture. Self-awareness and self-care are crucial to mastering the other aspects of becoming a computer athlete: Equipment and Usage, Nutrition, Strength and Conditioning, and Stress Management.

To become a computer athlete, develop your self-awareness and improve your habits and work environment through self-care.

A common pitfall plagues many computer users: they make assumptions about their pain and do not verify those assumptions. Even though they may spend more time on their computer than performing any other waking activity, when they experience pain, they assume that their pain is due to some other event or activity.

You can avoid unnecessary medical expenses and pain by not underestimating the effects of your computing habits and environment on your well-being.

Even I have been guilty of making this mistake. At one point, I developed chest pain on both the left and right sides of my chest. My first guess was that it was cold weather-related, or a cardiac or respiratory condition. Consequently, I visited my primary care physician and had several tests performed—including an EKG, a blood test, and a chest X-ray—as well as a physical examination. After all of these tests, my physician determined that I was in good health and offered to prescribe some anti-inflammatories or to refer me to a cardiologist. Needless to say, I had spent several hundred dollars in healthcare expenses using my high-deductible health plan and found myself without much to show for it.

Later, a coworker began complaining about his neck pain and assumed that even though his pain had begun just six months before, it was somehow due to a car accident he had been in two years ago. Reasoning that he was unlikely to have just started experiencing pain so recently from a car accident that had occurred two years ago, I offered to analyze his work environment. Not surprisingly, I found that he had situated his monitor in a way that required him to twist his neck to view the screen. When I brought this to his attention, he made some changes to his environment and adjusted his computer screen. I didn't hear anything about his neck pain after that.

After that, I began to seek an explanation for my own pain. I quickly realized that my pain came from using a Microsoft Natural keyboard. Although the natural keyboard allowed my wrists to remain in a neutral position, the narrow width of the keyboard relative to my shoulder width forced me to twist my shoulders inward like a chicken. I did some analysis and research on the internet and found a keyboard that could be adjusted to meet my needs and body proportions. I selected the Freestyle, made by Kinesis, because it was adjustable and had received a 2006 Ergonomics Expo award. After retiring my Microsoft Natural Keyboard and adding some additional strength and conditioning to my routine, my pain went away. I never had to reduce my computer usage. Had I looked first to my computing environment as the possible source of my pain, I would have avoided several months' worth of unnecessary expense, stress, and pain.

A key part of self-awareness and self-care is knowing your limits and not exceeding them. For example, if you know that you can only sit and work on a computer for 8 hours a day before it affects your productivity for the next day, you should try to avoid working beyond that threshold. If you can work productively for either 8 hours a day consistently or 12 hours one day and only 4 hours the next, you might as well work for 8 hours each day.

When you work past your threshold, you may cause physical damage to yourself: like sports injuries, computer-related injuries can recur and haunt you over time. For example, once you develop wrist pain, you may find that you reach your pain point much sooner whenever you perform the same behavior, even after rehabilitation.

Know your limits and do not exceed them.

There are many types of computer-related/repetitive stress injuries (RSI). Some examples: tendonitis or "trigger finger," carpal tunnel syndrome, thoracic outlet syndrome, and neck or back pain. Some injuries affect your nerves and are due to inflammation in your tendons or ligaments. I have personally had carpal tunnel, trigger finger, elbow pain, and chest/shoulder pain. At some points, using a computer became so painful that I could not use one at all.

Typically, these types of injuries do not creep up by surprise; in my case, these injuries had many warnings signs that I did not act on for several months or years. Some warning signs that you are developing a repetitive stress injury are musculoskeletal pain, numbness in your fingers, heat in your wrist, cracking noises in your wrist, and loss of grip strength or endurance. You may start to have trouble falling asleep because your body feels strange. Such insomnia tends to exacerbate the issue, causing you to become even more stressed out and less productive as your quality of sleep begins to suffer.

You can stop this cycle before your injury progresses to an advanced stage, and eliminate it—or at the very least prevent it from worsening—by becoming a computer athlete and beginning computer athlete rehabilitation.

If possible, identify and remedy the root cause of your injury, rather than just treating the symptoms. For example, if you have pain in your wrist because you rest your wrist on a hard surface while you type, you can take anti-inflammatories. The right approach, however, would be to change your habits and work environment so that you no longer rest your wrist on hard surfaces. Yet more often than not, we find that people either take anti-inflammatories or take no action. There are countless ways in which people treat the symptoms without fixing the root cause. A personal friend of mine owns a chiropractic and reflexology practice, and 70 percent of his clients come in for computer-related pain. If your pain is caused by leaning forward while working on the computer, getting a back adjustment by a chiropractor is not just expensive; it is also not going to fix the root cause. He expects to see his business from computer-related injuries increase as the number of people using a computer increases and as older populations spend more time on the computer.

Where possible, focus on and remedy the root cause of your discomfort.

Some people try to eliminate their computer use for a period of time, only to find that when they start using a computer again, their pain flares up once more. People wear wrist braces, stand up while using the computer, or resort to surgery or massage therapy. Many of these options have side effects, are expensive, and/or do not actually solve the problem or allow the person to compute in comfort.

On the other hand, there are situations in which treating the symptoms is the only viable course of action. For example, if you are allergic to pollen, you can either temporarily suppress the symptoms using allergy medicine or try something more extreme, such as staying indoors or wearing an astronaut suit. Most people just take allergy medicine. In general, I advocate being proactive, or at least reactive, to your pain and gradually making improvements to your work environment and habits that are aligned with becoming a computer athlete until you are able to use a computer in comfort.

Most of the effort required to become a computer athlete must be exerted by the individual. For example, it's possible to have the right equipment but still use it improperly and develop an injury. In fact, most of the things that contribute to computer-related injury are directly within your control. You can control the way you react to stress, the amount of sleep you get, and the amount and quality of food and water you consume, among other things.

It is important to realize that many of the health problems we face result from personal choices. Consider the staggering number of unhealthy people and the rising cost of healthcare in the United States. Roughly 10 percent of all healthcare costs in the U.S. are directly or indirectly related to diabetes. A large percentage of this money is spent on Type II diabetes, which is caused by genetics, obesity, and the consumption of refined sugar. If you have high blood sugar, you can change your habits and exercise or take medication. Unfortunately, people sometimes make poor decisions and have poor eating and exercise habits that neither their physicians nor their employer can impel them to change. Recently, I attended a healthcare IT conference focused on reducing healthcare costs in the U.S. through consumer-directed healthcare. At lunch, we were each served a large piece of steak and a hefty slice of chocolate cake. Most of the attendees consumed their entire meal. How ironic that, even as we were attending a healthcare conference about individuals making better healthcare decisions, we were all making extremely poor health decisions at the lunch table. At the end of the day, each of us must take the initiative to attain the vision of a computer athlete.

The onus is on the individual to attain a state of pain-free computing.

Computer Athlete Rehab

If you are injured and on the path to recovery, keep in mind some important principles. It is important to build gradually back up to your previous computer usage while paying attention to whether you are experiencing pain and adjusting your environment and habits until the pain dissipates. Many times, people want to get better faster and, in their zeal, make the mistake of over-stretching or doing too much physical therapy when their body actually needs some time to rest and recuperate. As I said above, make sure to identify and address the root cause of your pain and take steps to prevent the injury or other injuries from occurring in the future. Finally, it can be helpful to seek medical attention and/or take anti-inflammatories for a short period of time while you are recuperating.

While recuperating from an injury, it is important to build up gradually to your normal amount of computer usage.

Cleanliness

Too often, computer users neglect the cleanliness of their work environment. Some individuals' keyboards harbor more germs than their toilet. Many computer users notice that hair, skin cells, food, and bacteria accumulate into a brown grime on their keyboards. Few people, however, actually bother to clean their keyboard regularly by using alcohol swaps and removing all dust and debris from their keys and mouse. As well, computers' screens and fans can become dusty over time; they need to be cleaned with a lint cloth or an air can, respectively. In order to maintain good health and maintain a professional, hygienic working environment, a computer athlete should regularly clean his or her equipment.

Computer Habits Checklist

Here is a list of questions that you can use to evaluate your lifestyle and computing habits:

1. Do you have healthy food and/or water within reach while you work?

2. Do you feel that you get enough sleep?

3. Do you have a keyboard with low key pressure and a reasonable activation curve?

4. Do you have a good chair?

5. Do you work out your entire body so that your muscles do not atrophy?

6. Is your monitor at arm's distance away?

7. Do you context-switch frequently between programs to try to increase productivity?

8. Do you pronate your hands in order to press Shift or Control and a key?

9. Do you use your small digits (e.g. pinky finger) to press the arrow keys?

10. Do you feel as though you mouse a lot?

11. Does the position of your mouse, keyboard, monitor, etc. allow you to keep your arms and body in neutral positions?

12. Do you feel that your mouse or keyboard is too far away or at the wrong height?

13. How does stress affect the way you use your computer?

14. How many hours a day do you spend on your computer?

15. Do you feel that you have an ergonomic setup at home and at work?

16. What could you do to improve your setup or habits?

7. Strength and Conditioning

Using a computer is akin to participating in an athletic event. Lengthy computer use requires long, grueling hours of focus, concentration, physical coordination, and work. The grueling nature of using a computer can be seen in the long hours of maintaining good posture, balance, and coordination it requires. Using a computer requires endurance of a kind similar to that required by athletic activities such as long-distance running, biking, or swimming. Just as with other physical activities, some movements work better than others—form is important. There is even a body of study dedicated to studying the usage of computers and other machines, called ergonomics. Ergonomics is analogous to kinesiology, which is the study of the anatomy, physiology, and mechanics of body movement, typically in reference to sports.

Using a computer all day can be a grueling and physically demanding activity.

I am not necessarily arguing that working on a computer all day is as difficult or rigorous as, say, running a mile in under four minutes. I would, however, argue that using a computer is a physical activity that induces fatigue and wear and tear on the body. Like any other physical activity, computer use requires preparation in the form of strength and conditioning, proper training, and special equipment suited to the needs of the participant. The notion of a computer athlete is based on the precept that using a computer requires special training, discipline, and skill, and that people who possess these attributes can indeed be classified as such. We can observe individuals and intuitively ascertain which one is the better computer athlete, just as we can compare two track athletes. Becoming a computer athlete requires investing time and perhaps money, energy, and discipline. The fruits of this commitment? Increased productivity and pain-free computing.

Becoming a computer athlete requires strength training and conditioning.

Becoming a computer athlete requires strength and conditioning. On the one hand, using a computer for eight hours a day, five days a week does not require an extreme amount of strength or endurance. On the other hand, leading a completely sedentary lifestyle with no exercise will lead to muscular atrophy, poor posture, poor health, and pain. You don't necessarily need to engage in special activities in order to become a computer athlete. You just need to satisfy your basic need for whole-body conditioning, including aerobic exercise, weight-lifting, and stretching, so that you can be a happy, healthy computer user. Smaller individuals with smaller frames (typical of many women) may need to focus additionally on strength training. In general, you can satisfy your needs through a variety of activities, including dancing, yoga, ballet, gymnastics, running, climbing, and numerous others. It is particularly important to make sure you work out your core, or stomach, muscles and your lower back in order to maintain good posture. Aerobic exercise offers many benefits as well, including increasing cardiovascular health and promoting blood flow, which can have assist in the healing process. Weight training can help relieve stress and develop muscles that might otherwise atrophy; in addition, weight training can provide the strength you need to suspend your arms and hands so that you do not need to rest them on a surface while using the computer.

One pitfall to avoid is focusing on one area to the neglect of others. For example, engaging in endurance training, such as running long distance exclusively and becoming extremely skinny, may cause you to develop pain while using the computer. I am able to meet my needs for physical conditioning by lifting weights three times a week, jogging, walking to work, and stretching in the gym. I have found that whenever I slack off on exercise, I begin to develop pain somewhere in my body.

In short, I advocate full-body fitness for the computer athlete.

In order to become a computer athlete, you may need to condition yourself and engage in specialized training. The training you will require will depend on your goals and needs. If you want to be able to use the computer for 12 hours a day on a regular basis, you will likely need more training than someone who wants to use the computer for just four hours a day. Some types of conditioning involve making lifestyle changes, including changing your eating habits or learning to manage stress better. Other types of training include learning (or relearning) how to use your computer's input devices in order to minimize the impacts of computer usage on your body.

Through training and by relearning how to use your computer, you can minimize the impact of computer usage on your body.

In addition to physical preparation, you can take steps to be mentally prepared for computing. First, as we will discuss later, managing and minimizing your stress and how you react to stress is extremely important. Second, by engaging in some physical activity, you will feel better in addition to all of the other benefits of exercise. Finally, in order to be able to focus and accomplish your goals, you need to have discipline. Whether you are at work or at home working on a side project, you need to manage your distractions and your tasks. You need to realize what you need to do yourself and what you can let others do, as well as when to ask for help. You need to train other people so that they can help you and share your workload with other people. There are many great books available that discuss how to get things done, as well as how to be persistent and overcome adversity. I have read several and have benefitted from the effort.

In conclusion, using a computer places significant demands on your body and mind. These demands can wear you down and lead to injury unless you take steps to deal with them. In order to deal with these demands, you can condition yourself through aerobic exercise, stretching, strength exercises, as well as by learning computer techniques and input devices as discussed in the Equipment and Usage section. As part of your mental preparation, you can devote time and energy to improve how you manage stress and focus on your objectives. In order to meet your strength and conditioning needs, be resourceful. You can work with a personal trainer, professional coach, join a team sport, or read self-help books such as this one.

The Computer Athlete's Handbook

8. Stress Management

As in sports and athletic events, your mental or psychological state of mind can have a big impact on the way you perform at your computer. Your state of mind can affect your performance in many ways. For example, under stress, you may press down on the keyboard harder, take fewer breaks, or type faster. Also, as described in the works of John Sarno, *Healing Back Pain: The Mind-Body Connection*, you may develop pain in your back, neck, or any other part of your body as the physical manifestation of emotional stress. In addition to pain, your body's natural responses to stress can cause the production of extra hormones such as cortisol that in the short term help you focus and work more efficiently but can cause your body harm in the long term, even leading in some cases to heart attacks or strokes. Consequently, a computer athlete takes steps to minimize the impact of stress so that he can be a healthy, happy computer user.

Under stress, many people change their work habits to become more efficient but cause themselves physical harm in the process. For example, when programmers are in the last throes of a project, they are sometimes said to be on a "death march," also known as "crunch time" in other industries. During that time, employees tend to work longer hours under high amounts of stress. In some cases, companies have even prolonged crunch time in order to squeeze more out of their current employees. Whether or not such practices are fair, under demanding work conditions, you still have personal choices to make. You can become a computer athlete and avoid debilitating injury, or you can change companies. From my personal experience at a startup company, I know that stock options (aka "the golden handcuffs") can keep you tied to your work in hopes of a big future payoff. In my case, I decided to focus on attaining pain-free computing.

Stress affects the way you work at your computer and impacts your body's systems.

Stress affects different individuals in various ways. For example, when you see a police car and you are speeding on the freeway, does your heart rate speed up? Can you imagine staying calm and not having this type of biological reaction when seeing a police car? In the long term, it could be better for your health to stay relaxed in more life situations.

Pain can be a manifestation of stress, and sometimes can be resolved by resolving stressful issues. An anecdotal example: a personal friend of mine, who introduced me to the work of John Sarno, developed chronic back pain that persisted through many types of physical therapy and medicinal regimens. By reading Sarno's works and applying his techniques of writing down the aspects of her life that caused her stress and seeking to minimize or avert them, she was able to free herself from chronic back pain. Sarno's approach is not intended to offer a one-size-fits-all solution for every patient with chronic back or body pain. If, however, your pain is caused by emotional stress, the best way to eliminate your pain may be to eliminate or manage the emotional stress causing your pain. The bottom line is that if you are experiencing pain, it may not be due to your physical environment or work habits. The root cause of your pain may be your reaction to emotional stress. You'll want to keep that in mind when doing your root cause analysis.

Mental stress can manifest itself in physical pain.

On the other hand, you can manage and leverage stress to your advantage. For example, I do not drink coffee or consume caffeine; however, I am alert when I am at work and am generally known for being intense. I accomplish this by satisfying my bodily needs for sleep and refreshment, as well as giving myself breaks when necessary. In addition, I embrace opportunities that require working quickly under stress, and do my best to let my body remain focused and attentive while not overly exerting or stressing myself out. I try to lead by example. I believe that in order to be good at managing human resources, you ought to be good at managing yourself. If you cannot motivate or compel yourself to work and achieve results, I don't believe you will be good at motivating others. On the other hand, you must also understand that what drives you may not drive other people in the same way, and you may need to make adjustments.

You can manage and leverage stress to achieve improved performance.

Avoid Over-Committing

In addition to controlling your stress, you can also take steps to minimize the stress you experience. First, you can avoid over-committing yourself. In college, I overcommitted myself by taking an internship during the semester that required 20 hours a week and lacked sufficient flexibility. Whenever school became more demanding, I felt quite stressed out, since I still needed to complete work obligations during a period of academic intensity. If I had had a flexible job that had allowed me to work fewer hours when I was busy with school, I would not have been as stressed out. Next, you can select a company or profession more aligned with the type of lifestyle you want to lead. For example, if you do not want to deal with large amounts of stress, you may not want to work in an emergency room; if you do not want to work long hours, you should not become a junior investment banker.

Emotional Stress

Finally, you can work on your interpersonal relationships to reduce and prevent stressful situations from occurring. For example, if fighting with your spouse, significant other, friend, or family causes you large amounts of stress, you should proactively try to avoid or resolve conflicts that tend to escalate from repeated arguments or patterns of behavior. Another personal example: when my mother received calls from work during the weekend, my father would argue that my mother worked too much and was not compensated fairly. My mother would push back and state that she had an important obligation to keep the store running and that my dad didn't understand. The argument would escalate and my father would tell my mother that she was married to her job. This same argument was repeated many times over the years. The point is that while arguing raised both my mother and father's blood pressure, they never took steps to resolve or mitigate the conflict. My mother could have found a non-intrusive way to handle the needs of the store over the weekends, while my father could have agreed to cut my mom some slack. For many, including myself, stress from interpersonal relationships and life dwarfs stress from work, and a lot of stress can be avoided by working on those interpersonal relationships.

Stress from life and personal relationships can exceed work stress and can impact your performance.

The bottom line is that you can identify the things in your life that cause you stress and take steps to proactively mitigate or avoid them.

Stress is Temptation

Even in a situation where you cannot necessarily eliminate the source of your stress, you can control the way you respond to it. For example, there are computer programs available that allow you to track how you use your computer, from how long you hold the mouse to how quickly you type. When you realize that you are pressing on the keys harder or more frequently than you normally do, you can change your behavior. In my experience, people tend to take fewer breaks, use non-ergonomic hand movements like pronation to increase their output, and context switch too frequently between programs when under stress. When I am under stress, I remind myself of other stressful situations that I have successfully navigated through and tell myself that my current situation is not much different. Fortunately, my current line of work is not a matter of life or death, and I can reassure myself that if I work a bit more slowly, the consequences will not be dire. In general, understanding how stress can tempt you to deviate from the principles of computer athleticism but not failing prey to that temptation can help you avoid injury.

Stress can tempt you to deviate from the principles of computer athleticism. The best way to avoid injury, however, is to stay true to those principles.

9. Objections

As you contemplate many of the changes described in this book, you will probably be able to come up with reasons why a particular technique will not work for you. The point, however, is not to see how many objections or excuses you can dredge up. The point is, instead, to find the necessary changes you need to make to become a computer athlete.

There are different strokes for different folks—while some of these changes, like using a foot pedal, may be too extreme for you, they will work for other people. In fact, the worst thing anyone can do is to make fun of people who use foot pedals, put their keyboard on their lap, or use some other unconventional technique to help themselves avoid computer-related pain. For example, when I worked at Microsoft as an intern, my mentor told a senior manager of Microsoft Office that I used Dvorak and a foot pedal. The manager was very surprised and commented, "Whoa, freak." Fortunately, I was used to people's initially negative reactions to my foot pedal or my explanation of the computer athlete idea. On the other hand, many other people have responded very positively to my techniques, including physicians, chiropractors, entrepreneurs, computer programmers, and especially the CEO and CTO of the company I worked for while writing this book.

So that you can meet people's skepticism with confidence, I will walk through several common objections raised about the techniques described in this book. Most objections are related to equipment and usage; stress management, strength and conditioning, nutrition, and self-awareness and self-care are not easily observable when you are at work.

When you are at work or in a social situation, you will inevitably be confronted with situations where your food preferences may get some attention. For example, if you chose not to drink coffee, energy drinks, or soda, or to eat unhealthy foods like pizza or donuts, people will undoubtedly be curious. For some reason, people are not surprised if you chose not to smoke, but if you don't drink alcohol they wonder if something is wrong with you. Likewise, people may wonder whether you won't eat pizza because you were previously overweight, you are lactose intolerant, or you have strange food preferences. I usually say that I enjoy eating pizza, donuts, and the like, but try to avoid them. In reality, I usually don't feel good after consuming caffeine, soda, or any food that contains a lot of sugar. I tell people that I don't feel good after the sugar high—they usually leave me alone after that.

Some of the biggest challenges and objections I have faced related to my changing keyboard layouts. Learning a new keyboard layout is a significant time investment, and there are many reasonable objections to such an effort. First, although you can change the keyboard layout easily in Windows, Mac, or Linux, most keyboards you can purchase are made with the QWERTY layout printed on them. You can overcome this by purchasing a keyboard in your layout of choice, buying a kit of stickers to relabel the keys, popping off and moving the keys around, or simply learning to touch type the new layout on a keyboard in the QWERTY layout.

In my case, I printed a copy of Dvorak and placed it near my desk for reference while I learned to touch type using Ten Thumbs Typing. I am also bi-layout and can type in either layout. I am, however, much faster in Dvorak and greatly prefer it to QWERTY.

After you have decided how to deal with the key labels, you need to deal with the fact that most computers you will encounter will be in QWERTY rather than your layout of choice. First, you must determine whether you can be bi-layout and how your productivity will be impacted by being on a computer that is set to something other than your favorite layout. Second, you must think about how often you will be on a computer that you cannot temporarily remap. If you spend 99.9% of your time on your own computer and you do not share a computer with anyone else, then this may be a minor issue. But this may not be the case for everyone.

For example, in college, I competed in programming competitions called ACM : International Collegiate Programming Contests. In those contests, three students share one computer and solve six programming problems in a five- to six-hour time period. Because my team took turns typing on the computer, we had to run a command to change the keyboard layout, which added some time and frustration. In the end, it did not make that much difference.

The bottom line is that changing your keyboard layout leads to large productivity gains but is extremely challenging. I know of only about 20 people who use non-QWERTY layouts, and the number of Dvorak and Colemak users is less than 1% of the total number of keyboard users. At the same time, I believe that non-QWERTY keyboard layouts will gain more support over time. As well as myself, other people—like Barbara Blackburn, the world typing speed record holder; Bram Cohen, the inventor of BitTorrent; and Matt Mullenweg, lead developer of WordPress—use Dvorak.

People also object to ergonomic vertical mouses. By design, they cannot be used by everyone. For example, if a computer is intended to be shared by the public and its mouse is a right-handed vertical mouse, installing an ergonomic mouse may discriminate against left-handed people. I don't necessarily have a good solution to this, as most vertical mouses offer separate right- and left-handed versions. It may just not be feasible to use a vertical mouse in this type of environment.

On the other hand, if you spend most of your time at your own workstation or are ambidextrous, the above may not be a problem for you. The great thing about a vertical mouse is that it is easy to learn, moderately inexpensive, and eliminates a lot of discomfort. For almost all computer users, I would recommend looking into non-standard mouses, especially vertical mouses that use your larger muscle groups and appendages to operate.

A general objection to all non-standard devices is that if you travel, you cannot bring your setup with you. For individuals who rarely travel, this is not a significant objection. However, if you are like me, you spend a significant amount of time (10 to 20 percent) away from your setup. You may need to use your computer on the train, on an airplane, in a hotel room, or in a remote office. You can bring some of your equipment with you, such as your keyboard, mouse, and foot pedal. It is unlikely, however, that you will have a good chair or a second monitor with you. You can try to minimize the amount of work in a suboptimal environment, create a makeshift setup, or buy additional equipment for a remote office.

When I am on the road, I bring my mouse, keyboard, and foot pedal with me. I typically have additional equipment (such as an additional monitor and a good chair) at a remote office. In addition, I stack my monitor or laptop on books, put my keyboard on my lap, and move furniture around to make my setup more ergonomic. All of these strategies allow me to be productive when in a hotel or in a remote office. On the other hand, I do not use my computer on the train or on the plane; I typically use that time to read, think, or do design work. I find that airplanes are way too cramped to allow me to work comfortably. As well, it is difficult to stay hydrated, eat well, or use a foot pedal on a plane. Trains are better, but typically the trays are too high to be used comfortably—and I prefer not to use the keyboard on my laptop or place my laptop on top of my reproductive organs. In sum, you will miss your setup when you are on the road, but there are things you can do to get by.

If you use your laptop at work and want to be truly mobile, you may not be able to take your devices with you. When you are away from your desk, you may be doing a presentation, taking notes in a meeting, or engaging in some other type of light computer use. In these situations, you may simply not need to bring devices like an external keyboard and mouse with you. When I need to do more intensive computer activities with a team, I sit at a desk with a good setup with my team behind me. If my teammates also need to use their computers at the same time, I use software that allows us to collaborate in real-time like GoToMeeting, LogMeIn, GoToMyPC, and so on.

In addition to logistical problems, people may object to the cost of making changes. First, there can be quite a bit of upfront cost when purchasing new equipment like a mouse, chair, keyboard, foot pedal, keyboard tray, and/or second monitor. Second, finding the right equipment can be time-consuming and error-prone. Third, learning to use a new layout or device can require a substantial investment of time. For all of these changes, the cost is on the front end and the dividends are paid over time. You will need to evaluate and justify which changes make sense for you.

Many of these changes require that you schedule a transition period. For example, when I learned Dvorak, I had to wait until my semester was over and I was on a break. When you are a student, there is always winter and summer break. After you graduate, however, breaks are few and far between. Therefore, learning a new layout can be quite difficult when you are already in the workforce and under deadlines. You may need to wait until you are between jobs, have a light work period, or are on a vacation to learn a new layout.

To work through this objection, let's consider the cost of *not* making changes. If you don't make changes to attain pain-free computing, you will likely experience more pain, develop a computer-related injury, and reduce your own productivity and appetite for work. At some point, you will likely purchase some medicine and/or wrist braces, receive some medical attention, and lose some productivity. Doctor's visits, trips to the chiropractor, living in pain, and lost productivity all have a significant cost in terms of time and money. Also, in the long term, you may end up making many of these changes anyway. Therefore, you should seriously consider expending the effort on the front end and avoiding injury.

The Computer Athlete's Handbook

Conclusion

Like many other problems we face, repetitive stress injury is a problem created by man. The computer, keyboard, and mouse are all man-made. Even computer science, which is the study of computing systems and computation, is the study of the artificial. Most importantly, the problem of computer-related injury was created by man and can be fixed by man. We can change our standards and conventions, though it's difficult. When people learn how to use the computer, they can likewise be taught about ergonomics and proper computer usage, and make the necessary changes.

As of 2008, the state of affairs in computing is tragic. Many people have lived in pain for 10 years or more before figuring out how to attain pain-free computing. Countless others have become disabled, undergone surgery, and/or changed jobs due to injury. Too many people are affected by computer-related injury and poor health. Sadly, without a sea change, this state of affairs will not improve.

On the other hand, I am extremely optimistic that man can adapt to or change his environment. Thanks to new technology, dramatic improvements can be made by improving or changing the way we interact with a computer. These innovations have the potential to make it easier to achieve pain-free computing. Even without new technology, we can change our habits and understand and work within the limitations of our current tools.

We can also increase public awareness of the problem. We can start media campaigns or educational campaigns through federal agencies or the school system to tackle the problem through education. Any training or education about computer-related injury will need to focus on personal growth and understanding people's personal needs—as I have said, there is no one-size-fits-all approach. Schools could teach alternate keyboard layouts, or at least mention to students that they exist. Just as students have the option of learning Spanish or French in school, students could be given the choice to learn QWERTY or DVORAK. Computer courses could discuss the human- computer interaction and demonstrate proper technique. These programs could directly and indirectly save billions of dollars and offer a great return on investment.

Currently, too many resources are tied up in treating easily curable problems. In Africa, millions of children die every year due to respiratory infections from burning coal instead of wood chips or some other fuel. Although it doesn't result in death, computer-related injury is a big problem, and it is one we can remedy. We can look forward to the day when fewer resources are wasted on treating easily avoidable conditions and disorders. Just like people buy compact fluorescent lightbulbs to reduce emissions and save the Earth, we can all do our part when it comes to enjoying pain-free computing.

    This book is not intended to contain all of the information you will need to become a computer athlete. It is merely a jumping-off point. I hope it has provided you with some knowledge of computer-related injury and provided you with some tips and suggestions for mitigating your own difficulties. For example, you can adjust your sleep schedule and eating habits based on the suggestions contained in this book. On the other hand, finding the right chair or keyboard is going to require some effort and research on your part. In addition, there are many other great books and resources available to help you in your quest. Become a computer athlete, and you will reap the benefits.